Astral Projection

The ultimate astral projection guide with tips and techniques for astral travel, discovering the astral plane, and having an out of body experience!

Table of Contents

Introduction 1
Chapter 1: So You Want to Learn to Do Astral Projection? 2
Chapter 2: Out-of-the-Body Experience 6
Chapter 3: Astral Projections and Dreams 10
Chapter 4: How to Cause Astral Travel 14
Chapter 5: Frequently Asked Questions 23
Conclusion 26

Introduction

I want to thank you and congratulate you for downloading the book, "Astral Projection".

This book contains helpful information about astral projection, what it is, and how you can begin practicing astral travel yourself!

Throughout this guide, you will learn about the history and beliefs surrounding astral projection. You will discover the benefits of astral travel, and better understand how astral projection works.

You will be given step by step instructions that will help you to experience astral travel for yourself. While these can take practice, usually astral projection can be experienced within just 1 month of using these techniques!

This book also contains a 'frequently asked questions' section that will answer the most common questions in relation to astral projection, including the dangers of astral travel, and how to stay safe.

Overall, astral projection is a fun and enriching experience, I am glad that you have decided to take the time to experience this phenomena for yourself, and wish you the best of luck!

Thanks again for downloading this book, I hope you enjoy it!

Chapter 1:
So You Want to Learn to Do Astral Projection?

Psychic reading, telepathy, clairvoyance, astral projection, and outside the body experience, among others, are "subjects" that science has no direct definition and proof of. There is a whole "new world" outside what our naked eyes can see. There are things that we cannot explain or define as exact science.

One of the most popular subjects is astral projection. People say that astral projection happens when your spiritual self leaves your physical. Is it really possible to have an out of body experience? How does this happen? Would you be aware if you experience it? These questions will be answered throughout this book.

What is Astral Projection?

Astral projection is also referred to as astral travel. Simply put, it is a spiritual interpretation of an out-of-body-experience. It is a phenomenon wherein your consciousness "leaves" your physical body while still being connected through a "silver cord".

Astral projection is often associated with reaching a meditative state. Your astral body moves out of your physical and travels around the astral plane (more about this in the succeeding chapters).

You can do astral travel while you are awake, in deep meditation, or lucid dreaming. Those who have experienced an outside-the-body-experience attest that their spiritual body moves around the spirit world during astral travel. The concept of astral travel has been around for thousands of years, but it remains a controversial topic because scientists have yet to find physical proof of astral travel.

General Schools of Thoughts on Astral Projection:

Phasing Model – According to Robert Monroe, it is not possible to literally leave your body and the physical world and astral planes are just points in the endless spectrum of your consciousness. When you project, you are brought to a different area of consciousness. This is quite similar to turning the dial of your radio to tune in to a different radio station. One of the first signposts that represent this change of phase is referred to as the state of focus 10, which is the state of a conscious mind and body that is asleep.

Mystical Model – This includes a wide array of astral maps and belief systems that are all tied together by their belief that astral travel occurs outside a person's actual physical body. There is a more subtle energy that is said to carry the consciousness outside of your physical body, connected by an energy that can be "seen" as a silver cord similar to an umbilical cord.

Types of Astral Projection

Different types of astral projection have been identified based on the lucidity level and energetic control that you will experience. Here are a few of them:

- Spontaneous Projections

    These are unplanned projections. They are often out of the control of the person who experiences it. These projections happen when someone has a predisposition for some degree of bio-energetic (chi or prana) "looseness". This means that the energy system of the people who experience it is like water which flows freely.

Spontaneous projections can occur while you are taking a nap or you are sleeping through the night. While your body is asleep, you will suddenly find yourself outside your physical body. There might be cases wherein you will see your physical body while in the sleeping position.

- Forced Projections

   A sudden trauma to the body, like being involved in a car accident, may cause these sudden projections from your physical body.

   The people who have experienced such projections say that they suddenly found themselves lucidly watching their physical body. Projections happen suddenly and those who experience them are startled with each occurrence.

- Unconscious Projections

   Have you ever had that feeling of sinking then suddenly waking up with a jolt? Experts say that this could be a momentary out-of-body experience. When these types of projections occur, your body is separated from your physical body by a few inches. It usually occurs during your sleep state.

   Your astral body may hover just above your physical body, attached by the silver cord. When this happens naturally, your astral body is recharged with the energy it needs.

- Semi-Lucid Projections

    These projections often leave bits and pieces of memories that you are able to recall. During the experience, you may go back and forth dreaming and projecting, but never actually reaching the state of full awareness or full lucidity.

    You may also experience blackout episodes followed by un-lucid periods or semi-lucid periods.

- Fully-Lucid Projections

    While you are experiencing astral travel, you are fully conscious and aware of what is happening. You are able to control your thoughts and energies. This may occur with or without you consciously taking off from your physical body.

Chapter 2:
Out-of-the-Body Experience

Here are important terms to remember about astral projection. The following will help you further understand what this subject is all about.

Astral Body

When you are dreaming, you often experience out-of-the-body projections to the astral plane. When you dream, it is highly likely that you will not be able to remember what you dreamt of, much more so if you had an out-of-the-body experience.

The astral body is the intermediate body between your spiritual body (spirit) and your physical body. It is lighter than your physical body and highly "changeable". It has more density and shape than your pure spirit. While your astral body appears like your human form, it can change its appearance, shift shapes, and it can even pass through walls.

Astral Plane

The astral plane, or simply known as 'the astral', is that world between the spiritual and physical world. There are many different astral planes and we move through them in our dreams.

As human beings, we reside in the physical plane, where our consciousness focuses and we are aware of the things around us. We are actually multidimensional. Each one of us has parts of ourselves in a variety of planes. However, to survive in the physical plane, our subconscious mind has to ignore all the other planes, for example, the one reading this book is in its human form.

You, for instance, are a man (or a woman) in flesh and blood, or you can say that you are a soul manifested in a human body.

The inhabitants actually generate the physical plane, meaning, you create your own experiences with your feelings, emotions, and beliefs. Many things are specific only to the physical plane and all the other planes follow other rules.

Take note that all planes are unique from one another. Astral travelers are known to be in at least two planes, astral and physical. Experts say that the astral plane is considered a mere extension of the physical plane. It is some sort of an access point to all the other planes.

There are seven dimensions in the astral plane, each corresponding to the seven divisions of matter: solid, liquid, gas, etheric, super-etheric, subatomic, and atomic. They play major roles in the destiny of human beings. Briefly, here are the seven dimensions of the astral world:

7th Astral Dimension

This is the lowest dimension of the astral world, and is known as the *Avichi*. This is where the unrestrained passions reside. The astral body has the same dense matter, as well. To be in this dimension is to be in "hell".

This is actually the place of existence where your innermost desires are not met because you do not have the physical body to make them into reality.

6th Astral Dimension

There is very little difference between physical existence and the lower subdivision of the lower sub-plane. When you find yourself in this plane, you will recognize familiar surroundings with the people you once met.

The higher sub-planes of the 6th dimension will find the inhabitants to be living in a world that they have made.

5th Astral Dimension

The inhabitants of the 5th dimension are busy with their own intellectual desires. They are working towards the aspirations that they were not able to manifest in their physical plane.

4th Astral Dimension

In this dimension, the inhabitants and sceneries are those people living out the lives they had in their earthly life. They have created their own world, the ones that they have enjoyed.

3rd Astral Dimension

The dwellers are productive here. They are working on their craft and creating masterpieces that they cannot create in the physical life.

2nd Astral Dimension

This is actually not a place, but a region. The inhabitants of this plane are diverse: from all walks of life that have different beliefs. This is where religious aspirations and emotions are fully expressed.

1st Astral Dimension

This is the highest of the planes of the astral word. This is where the great scientists, metaphysicians, and philosophers reside.

Astral Travel

In the astral world, there is a more fluid existence compared to the physical world. There are no limitations to what you can do as you travel into the astral world. You can actually go from one dimension to another and travel back to the past or into the future. This is also where people find it easier to communicate with their deceased loved ones.

You can travel into dimensions that you did not know existed.

Chapter 3:
Astral Projections and Dreams

The astral body can perform a lot of tasks, for example it can create new events and developments that have yet to manifest in your physical world. You can liken the astral plane to a huge laboratory wherein you can conduct a variety of experiments in your life and in your "creations".

This is a place where you can also view things from a different perspective. Your dream experiences in the astral plane will allow you to see things from a different angle, thus, giving you another point of view. This will be useful when there are decisions that you need to make or there are challenges that you do not know how to face. By seeing things differently, even if they are only "astral dream experiences", you get the chance to weigh in alternative solutions to the dilemma that you have.

Learning Astral Travel through Dreaming

Before you can learn to do astral traveling, you need to begin remembering your dreams. You can do this by having a blank piece of paper and a pen on your bedside table. Before sleeping, tell yourself that you will be dreaming and that you will be able to remember your dream when you wake up.

In the morning, when you start to stir, continue to lay still and with your eyes closed, try to recall whatever you have dreamt about that night. Write everything down, even the most insignificant details that you can recall.

What to take note of? You might have been with some people in your dream or you were in a particular place, or you might have been something. Make sure you indicate the date. Continue to do this every night. Maybe, instead of writing on a piece of paper, you can write them down in your journal or even an ordinary notebook. It does not matter where you write them down. The important thing is that you are able to keep track of your dreams.

Do not worry if you cannot remember everything all at once, it takes a lot of practice and patience. It may take you a few weeks to a month before you are able to recall dreams more spontaneously. With constant practice, you will be recalling your dreams easily.

Here is a helpful note: If you need to set an alarm to wake up when you need to go to work, do not use a buzzer, and use music instead. A buzzer may be too abrupt and stressful, and will inhibit your ability to remember your dreams.

Experts say that everyone does astral travel while dreaming. When you are having a feeling of De-Ja-vu, it only means that you have been in that particular place or experienced that exact thing in your dreams. If you do not have a dream journal, you would not be able to recall that you have dreamt it.

It is important that you maintain a dream journal and leave blank spaces per day so that you can make entries later on about what the dream meant. Some people consult psychics to have their dreams interpreted. If you are going this route, then a dream journal would be most helpful.

Astral Traveling

When you have learned how to recall dreams, it's time to learn how to astral travel.

Make sure you are dressed comfortably and in a comfortable position, you can either lie down or sit back. Set the room's lighting to low. Remove a watch or anything metal that you are wearing. You also have to make sure that there will be no sudden noises that could wake you up.

If initially you are not confident in doing this alone, then ask someone to be there with you in case you will need to be awakened. That person will just quietly be there with you and look for signs that you need help in coming back.

Close your eyes and begin to relax. Concentrate on your toes, then stretch and release. Move to your legs, stretch and release. Do this for the entire body until you reach the crown of your head.

By this time, you are beginning to quiet the mind and your breathing has become slower. This will put you in complete relaxation.

You have now reached the meditative state and you are ready to concentrate on an image, any image that comes to mind. Allow this image to expand and to flow until it takes on different movements, followed by more images. Soon, you will see images flashing as if you are watching a movie. Keep calm and let the images flash, remember this is just a movie and the images won't hurt you.

You will reach a deeper relaxation state and your mind will become clearer. Observe your surroundings without opening your eyes. Keep looking and soon you'll see a pattern of lights, but it will disappear and you will only see things through your "third eye". The images that you will be seeing will be through your "intuitive eye" only.

During this time, you have become unaware of your body. This is the state that you have to be in before you "leave" your body.

You will soon be entering a state of vibration, which is an important state because astral travel is all about vibration. You may feel a slight tingling sensation. This means, you are beginning to leave your body.

Initially, allow a little separation of yourself to emerge from your crown chakra. It is important that you control your vibrational state. Allow energy to flow out of your crown chakra, then bring it back and send it to your toes. Practice until you are able to control your spiritual body and you will be ready for astral travel.

Dissociate from your body through your crown chakra. Imagine that you are getting lighter and lighter once you are in your vibrational state. Imagine flying and floating, feel how wonderful it is to float upward into the sky. During this time, your mind has to stay clear from any kind of thoughts.

You are now having an out-of-the-body experience. Since you are doing this for the first time, do not make drastic moves. Just explore something close by, like the room next to yours. Once you have explored a few areas around your house, return to where you left your body and enter back in.

Do not attempt to travel for more than five minutes until you have practiced long enough. As a beginner, it is ideal to start with baby steps. It is natural to feel fear for the unknown, but with constant practice, you will be astral traveling without too much of an effort.

The next chapter will give you more techniques on how to do astral traveling effectively.

Chapter 4:
How to Cause Astral Travel

Astral Projection and Fear

As briefly mentioned in the previous chapter, it is normal to get a feeling of fear of astral traveling. Have you ever experienced having perceptions or sensations while sleeping or when you are about to fall asleep? It is a feeling of uneasiness and fear, and you do not know where it's coming from. You may have experienced having nightmares or sleep paralysis, or you may have heard or saw something unusual.

This may be "projectiophobia" or the fear of astral projection. Technically, it is a fear of out-of-the-body-experience, including subtle dimensions and non-physical beings.

This is a natural reaction. People experience different intensities when it comes to out-of-the-body experience. This fear prevents people from exploring this subject matter.

Common Causes of Fear of Astral Projection

- Most people are afraid of getting lost and not being able to return to their physical body.

- Most fear about the silver cord being cut and they will eventually die.

- They are afraid that someone else might get to their physical body and they will not be able to go back to their own bodies.

- They are afraid to venture into unknown and mysterious planes.

These are natural emotions, but you have to learn to master them instead of them mastering you. Take control of your thoughts to take control of your reality. The challenge lies in understanding your own emotions and letting them emerge for you to have a better understanding of yourself.

Today may be a good day to start.

Astral Projection without Fear

Face your fears! Facing your fear is part of the learning process of this life. Each one of us is "consciousness" (spirits, souls) and we all have lived in different lifetimes. Our continual rebirth will help provide us the opportunities to experience a variety of situations that will eventually help us to learn the things we are supposed to learn.

Most of the areas and the skills that we need to improve on are simply the areas that we need to experience further in order to deal with them accordingly.

What are you most afraid of about astral traveling? The truth is, your fear won't disappear until you have faced the "challenge".

Your greatest fear can become your greatest strength, you just have to learn how to recognize and develop it.

Other Considerations

Everyone has his or her own blind spots, meaning we all have traits in our personalities that we are unaware of. It remains "unseen" and incomprehensible.

Think about it, you cannot work on what you cannot see. Don't expect change because it is not going to happen. This is the reason why people suffer; it is because of their ignorance about the blind spots because they actually do not know that these exist.

Consequently, when you are able to see and understand, the more you can work on improving them. This is the reason why some people deny their fears (though unconsciously) and simply keep them as blind spots.

The more you gain experiences, the more you become mature and feel stronger to face whatever fears and challenges that might come your way.

Throughout the course of history, paranormal phenomenon has had an aura of suspicion surrounding it, mostly because we simply lack the necessary information to understand it. The good news is that these modern times have given us many things to help us better understand this phenomena and why it occurs.

Replace fear with knowledge. Replace imagination with research. If there is anything to fear, then you have to learn to face it, and a great place to face fears is through astral travel.

Techniques to Perform Astral Projection

This section will teach you how to do astral travel.

Preparing Yourself

1. **Begin in the morning**. Experts recommend that it is better to practice astral projection in the morning rather than doing it at night. Instead of practicing right before you fall asleep, try doing it in the early hours of the morning, when you are still feeling drowsy. You will

find it easier to reach a deeper state of relaxation and heightened awareness hours before the sun goes up.

2. **Create the perfect atmosphere.** When you are doing astral travel, you need to enter into a deep state of relaxation; hence, it is better to do this preferably in your room where you are most comfortable. Lie down on your bed and begin to relax your mind and body.

It is advisable to perform astral projection alone rather than with someone else in the room. If you are just starting to do this and you are not confident yet, you can ask someone to be there in the room in case you begin to panic or you need to wake up. Otherwise, perform it alone. If you sleep with your partner beside you, find a room where you can do astral projection on your own, an area in the house that is still comfortable and with minimal noise.

Draw the curtains and turn off the light. Any form of interruption can disrupt the process so make sure that there won't be any.

3. **Lie down on your back and relax.** Find a comfortable position, whether lying down or sitting up straight. Just make sure you are comfortable. Close your eyes. Clear your mind from any distracting thoughts. Concentrate on your own body. Feel every part of your body and be aware of each part. Your main purpose here is to reach a state of complete relaxation of the body and mind.

Flex your muscles to loosen them. Similar to what the previous chapter instructed, start with your toes all the way up to your head. There is no need to rush. Just make sure that every muscle in your body is relaxed.

Practice slow and deep breathing. Inhale deeply and exhale completely. Relax and refrain from holding tension in your chest and shoulders. Just let go!

Focus on every breath you take. Do not think about the things you need to accomplish for the day or the important meeting you have to prepare for, or how you can get money to pay for the mortgage. Do not let negative thoughts control and prevent you from reaching deep relaxation and calmness. Free your mind and your body so that your soul can begin projecting itself.

Allow yourself to "get lost" in deep relaxation.

Dissociating from your Body

1. **Aim to reach the hypnotic state.** The hypnotic state is also referred to as the "hypnagogic" state. Go to that state where you are about to fall asleep, without completely falling asleep and losing consciousness. The hypnotic state is the state where you are just at the edge of wakefulness and sleep. This is necessary for you to do astral travel.

    Reach the hypnotic state with the following steps:

    - With your eyes closed, allow your mind to wander to any part of your body, like a single toe, your foot, or your hand.

    - Focus on that particular part until you are able to see it clearly without literally seeing it. Continue doing it with your eyes closed. Keep on focusing until you completely keep away every thought whether positive or negative.

- Using only your mind, flex that particular body part you chose. Do not physically move in. Instead, visualize the actions. Imagine seeing your toes curling and uncurling or your fingers clenching and unclenching.

- Now, broaden the focus to the rest of the body. Using the same technique, move your feet, your legs, your fingers, your hands, until you reach your head. You do so only in your mind. Maintain your focus until you are moving your entire body with the use of your mind alone.

2. **Go into a state of vibration.** This is the part where most people begin to feel afraid because the waves of vibration will come in varying frequencies. This is crucial because this state will prepare your soul to leave your body. Do not be like most people who fear vibrations. If you become afraid, you might not be able to enter the meditative state completely. You might end up succumbing to the vibrations as you begin to prepare your soul to dissociate from your physical body.

3. **Use mind control to move your astral body from your physical body.** Picture in your mind the room where you are right that moment. See yourself in your mind moving and preparing to stand up. Look around the room and get off the bed. Walk around your room and look back at your physical body.

You have successfully dissociated your astral body from your physical body if you are able to feel yourself gazing at yourself in bed. As you gaze around the room, you will realize that your conscious body is finally out of your physical body.

It may take a lot of practice to reach this point. If you find it hard to lift your astral body away from your physical body completely, then start small, like lifting your hands or legs first, but not the entire body.

You will need constant practice so do not worry if during the first few days, you are still lifting parts of your body instead of the whole body. Keep on practicing until you can move around the room.

4. **Go back to your physical body.** As previously stated, your physical body and your astral body remain connected to each other by an invisible force referred to as the silver cord. This force will guide your astral body back to where you left your physical body. Re-enter your body. Move your body starting from the toes and fingers, make sure you move it physically; you will slowly regain full consciousness in a few minutes.

Exploration of the Astral Plane

1. **Verify if you are actually projecting your astral body (or your soul) from your physical body.** When you have constantly practiced and mastered the act of astral projection within the same room, you will need confirmation that you were able to reach two separate planes.

How do you do that?

> ➤ Next time you do astral travel do not look back at your physical body. Just leave the room and walk to another area in your house.

> ➤ When you are in another room, examine an object that you will find inside the room. Choose something that you have not actually noticed before when you are in your physical body. Take note of the details, like the color, size and shape of the object. If you can take note of as many details as possible, the better.

> ➤ Now, go back to your room and return to your physical body. When you are back, get up and walk to the room you visited during astral travel. Go towards the object you have examined. Are you able to see the same details that you have seen while astral travelling?

2. **Explore some more.** The astral plane is a whole new world waiting for you to explore. In your succeeding astral projections, visit places that are unfamiliar to you and every time, take note of details that you have not seen or noticed in the past. After every astral projection session, physically see if the details you took note of are accurate.

3. **Go back to the body.** There are people who say that astral travel is dangerous and risky, especially when you do not have enough practice in going to unfamiliar locations.

Before doing astral projection, picture yourself bathing in glowing, white light. Picture this light as a cloud around you. This will help protect you from outside and unnecessary thoughts.

While there are people who are skeptics, the sheer thrill of traveling outside of your body is enough for them to practice and explore some more.

Notes:

Do not worry about the silver cord being broken because it won't. However, according to experts and astral travelers, it is possible to delay the astral body from going back into physical body if a person spends too much energy outside of the physical body.

Some people fear that demonic forces might take advantage of their physical body and inhabit it. If you are worrying about this, you can protect yourself by having the room blessed before you begin with astral projection.

It is possible for your astral body to interact with other astral bodies. Ask a friend to try it with you or you can ask your partner to do it together. Some people also say that astral sex is a mind-blowing activity. Be sure to go back to your body, though.

Chapter 5:
Frequently Asked Questions

1. **How long does it take for one to have an out-of-the-body experience?**

   Some people can do spontaneous astral traveling, meaning they can experience it without much preparation or application of different techniques. These are the people who may have done extensive practice or have accumulated many psychic experiences.

   For the average person, there is a training process wherein they can try different techniques until they're able to do astral projection successfully. It is important that you find a technique that you will be most comfortable with and that fits your personality.

   You may apply some existing techniques, but you need to create your own routine. The best form of practice is doing it every day for at least 20 to 30 minutes. Consider it learning a new skill and you need to constantly practice in order to master it.

2. **How will I know exactly when I am having an out-of-the-body-experience?**

   There are a few indications, like experiencing an energetic shower or a strong yet pleasant sensation of energy flowing throughout your body the moment you wake up. This happens because your astral body collected various energies while floating around.

3. **How can I control the vibrational state?**

   The vibrational state is an energetic technique. It is controlled by your own will. In order to control it, you need to apply personal organization and will to be able to schedule the technique at least 20 times a day. You will need to set up an alarm every 40 minutes during the day, and at this time focus on feeling the vibrational energy.

4. **Can children have OBE's?**

   It is not common but it can happen, especially if a child is para-psychic and can interact with other dimensions. Some psychics attest to having experiences during childhood that helped develop their psychic ability.

   While it is not common, it will not hurt to watch out for signs.

5. **How can I benefit from astral projection?**

   Most people say that astral projection has helped them recall their past life and they were able to remember a few mistakes that had dire consequences. In so doing, they are able to learn about the lessons without having to experience the same in this lifetime.

   In addition, there are those who attest to having improved sleeping habits. They also became more productive and more assertive in expressing themselves.

   Overall, most of the people who practice astral projection say that their lives have improved as a result. While it may not be for everyone, astral projection is usually an enriching experience, that I encourage you to try for yourself!

Conclusion

Thank you again for downloading this book!

I hope this book was able to help you learn more about astral projection!

The next step is to put this information to use, and begin practicing astral projection yourself!

Finally, if you enjoyed this book, please take the time to share your thoughts and post a review on Amazon. It'd be greatly appreciated!

Thank you and good luck!